LEONARD BERNSTEIN
VARIATIONS ON AN OCTATONIC SCALE

Recorder and Cello

ISBN 978-1-4584-1761-9

7777 W. BLUEMOUND RD. P.O. BOX 13819 MILWAUKEE, WI 53213

www.leonardbernstein.com
www.boosey.com
www.halleonard.com

LEONARD BERNSTEIN
August 25, 1918 – October 14, 1990

Leonard Bernstein was born in Lawrence, Massachusetts. He took piano lessons as a boy and attended the Garrison and Boston Latin Schools. At Harvard University he studied with Walter Piston, Edward Burlingame-Hill, and A. Tillman Merritt, among others. Before graduating in 1939 he made an unofficial conducting debut with his own incidental music to *The Birds*, and directed and performed in Marc Blitzstein's *The Cradle Will Rock*. Subsequently, at the Curtis Institute of Music in Philadelphia, he studied piano with Isabella Vengerova, conducting with Fritz Reiner, and orchestration with Randall Thompson.

In 1940 he studied at the Boston Symphony Orchestra's newly created summer institute, Tanglewood, with the orchestra's conductor, Serge Koussevitzky. Bernstein later became Koussevitzky's conducting assistant.

Bernstein was appointed to his first permanent conducting post in 1943, as Assistant Conductor of the New York Philharmonic. On November 14, 1943, Bernstein substituted on a few hours notice for the ailing Bruno Walter at a Carnegie Hall concert, which was broadcast nationally on radio, receiving critical acclaim. Soon orchestras worldwide sought him out as a guest conductor.

In 1945 he was appointed Music Director of the New York City Symphony Orchestra, a post he held until 1947. After Serge Koussevitzky died in 1951, Bernstein headed the orchestral and conducting departments at Tanglewood, teaching there for many years. In 1951 he married the Chilean actress and pianist, Felicia Montealegre. He was also visiting music professor, and head of the Creative Arts Festivals at Brandeis University in the early 1950s.

Bernstein became Music Director of the New York Philharmonic in 1958. From then until 1969 he led more concerts with the orchestra than any previous conductor. He subsequently held the lifetime title of Laureate Conductor, making frequent guest appearances with the orchestra. Over half of Bernstein's more than 400 recordings were made with the New York Philharmonic.

Bernstein traveled the world as a conductor. Immediately after World War II, in 1946, he conducted in London and at the International Music Festival in Prague. In 1947 he conducted in Tel Aviv, beginning a relationship with Israel that lasted until his death. In 1953, Bernstein was the first American to conduct opera at the Teatro alla Scala in Milan in Cherubini's *Medea* with Maria Callas.

Bernstein was a leading advocate of American composers, particularly Aaron Copland. The two remained close friends for life. As a young pianist, Bernstein performed Copland's *Piano Variations* so often he considered the composition his trademark. Bernstein programmed and recorded nearly all of the Copland orchestral works — many of them twice. He devoted several televised *Young People's Concerts* to Copland, and gave the premiere of Copland's *Connotations*, commissioned for the opening of Philharmonic Hall (now Avery Fisher Hall) at Lincoln Center in 1962.

While Bernstein's conducting repertoire encompassed the standard literature, he may be best remembered for his performances and recordings of Haydn, Beethoven, Brahms, Schumann, Sibelius and Mahler. Particularly notable were his performances of the Mahler symphonies with the New York Philharmonic in the 1960s, sparking a renewed interest in the works of Mahler.

Inspired by his Jewish heritage, Bernstein completed his first large-scale work as a composer, Symphony No. 1: "Jeremiah" (1943). The piece was first performed with the Pittsburgh Symphony Orchestra in 1944, conducted by the composer, and received the New York Music Critics' Award. Koussevitzky premiered Bernstein's Symphony No. 2: "The Age of Anxiety" with the Boston Symphony Orchestra, with Bernstein as piano soloist. His Symphony No. 3: "Kaddish," composed in 1963, was premiered by the Israel Philharmonic Orchestra. "Kaddish" is dedicated "To the Beloved Memory of John F. Kennedy."

Other major compositions by Bernstein include *Prelude, Fugue and Riffs* for solo clarinet and jazz ensemble (1949); *Serenade* for violin, strings and percussion (1954); *Symphonic Dances from West Side Story* (1960); *Chichester Psalms* for chorus, boy soprano and orchestra (1965); *Mass: A Theater Piece for Singers, Players and Dancers*, commissioned for the opening of the John F. Kennedy Center for the Performing Arts in Washington, DC, and first produced there in 1971; *Songfest*, a song cycle for six singers and orchestra (1977); *Divertimento*, for orchestra (1980); *Halil*, for solo flute and small orchestra (1981); *Touches*, for solo piano (1981); *Missa Brevis* for singers and percussion (1988); *Thirteen Anniversaries* for solo piano (1988); *Concerto for Orchestra: Jubilee Games* (1989); and *Arias and Barcarolles* for two singers and piano duet (1988).

Bernstein also wrote a one-act opera, *Trouble in Tahiti*, in 1952, and its sequel *A Quiet Place* in 1983. He collaborated with choreographer Jerome Robbins on three major ballets: *Fancy Free* (1944) and *Facsimile* (1946) for the American Ballet theater; and *Dybbuk* (1975) for the New York City Ballet. He composed the score for the award-winning movie *On the Waterfront* (1954) and incidental music for two Broadway plays: *Peter Pan* (1950) and *The Lark* (1955).

Bernstein contributed substantially to the Broadway musical stage. He collaborated with Betty Comden and Adolph Green on *On The Town* (1944) and *Wonderful Town* (1953). In collaboration with Richard Wilbur and Lillian Hellman and others he wrote *Candide* (1956). Other versions of *Candide* were written in association with Hugh Wheeler, Stephen Sondheim, et al. In 1957 he again collaborated with Jerome Robbins, Stephen Sondheim, and Arthur Laurents, on the landmark musical *West Side Story*, also made into the Academy Award-winning film. In 1976 Bernstein and Alan Jay Lerner wrote *1600 Pennsylvania Avenue*.

Festivals of Bernstein's music have been produced throughout the world. In 1978 the Israel Philharmonic sponsored a festival commemorating his years of dedication to Israel. The Israel Philharmonic also bestowed on him the lifetime title of Laureate Conductor in 1988. In 1986 the London Symphony Orchestra and the Barbican Centre produced a Bernstein Festival. The London Symphony Orchestra in 1987 named him Honorary President. In 1989 the city of Bonn presented a Beethoven/Bernstein Festival.

In 1985 the National Academy of Recording Arts and Sciences honored Mr. Bernstein with the Lifetime Achievement Grammy Award. He won eleven Emmy Awards in his career. His televised concert and lecture series started with the *Omnibus* program in 1954, followed by the extraordinary *Young People's Concerts with the New York Philharmonic* in 1958 that extended over fourteen seasons. Among his many appearances on the PBS series *Great Performances* was the acclaimed eleven-part "Bernstein's Beethoven." In 1989, Bernstein and others commemorated the 1939 invasion of Poland in a worldwide telecast from Warsaw.

Bernstein's writings were published in *The Joy of Music* (1959), *Leonard Bernstein's Young People's Concerts* (1961), *The Infinite Variety of Music* (1966), and *Findings* (1982). Each has been widely translated. He gave six lectures at Harvard University in 1972-1973 as the Charles Eliot Norton Professor of Poetry. These lectures were subsequently published and televised as *The Unanswered Question*.

Bernstein always rejoiced in opportunities to teach young musicians. His master classes at Tanglewood were famous. He was instrumental in founding the Los Angeles Philharmonic Institute in 1982. He helped create a world class training orchestra at the Schleswig Holstein Music Festival. He founded the Pacific Music Festival in Sapporo, Japan. Modeled after Tanglewood, this international festival was the first of its kind in Asia and continues to this day.

Bernstein received many honors. He was elected in 1981 to the American Academy of Arts and Letters, which gave him a Gold Medal. The National Fellowship Award in 1985 applauded his life-long support of humanitarian causes. He received the MacDowell Colony's Gold Medal; medals from the Beethoven Society and the Mahler Gesellschaft; the Handel Medallion, New York City's highest honor for the arts; a Tony award (1969) for Distinguished Achievement in the Theater; and dozens of honorary degrees and awards from colleges and universities. He was presented ceremonial keys to the cities of Oslo, Vienna, Bersheeva and the village of Bernstein, Austria, among others. National honors came from Italy, Israel, Mexico, Denmark, Germany (the Great Merit Cross), and France (Chevalier, Officer and Commandeur of the Legion d'Honneur). He received the Kennedy Center Honors in 1980.

World peace was a particular concern of Bernstein. Speaking at Johns Hopkins University in 1980 and the Cathedral of St. John the Divine in New York in 1983, he described his vision of global harmony. His "Journey for Peace" tour to Athens and Hiroshima with the European Community Orchestra in 1985, commemorated the 40th anniversary of the atom bomb. In December 1989 Bernstein conducted the historic "Berlin Celebration Concerts" on both sides of the Berlin Wall, as it was being dismantled. The concerts were unprecedented gestures of cooperation, the musicians representing the former East Germany, West Germany, and the four powers that had partitioned Berlin after World War II.

Bernstein supported Amnesty International from its inception. To benefit the effort in 1987, he established the Felicia Montealegre Fund in memory of his wife who died in 1978.

In 1990 Bernstein received the Praemium Imperiale, an international prize created in 1988 by the Japan Arts Association and awarded for lifetime achievement in the arts. Bernstein used the $100,000 prize to establish initiatives in the arts and education, principally the Leonard Bernstein Center for Artful Learning.

Bernstein was the father of three children — Jamie, Alexander, and Nina — and the grandfather of two: Francisca and Evan.

VARIATIONS ON AN OCTATONIC SCALE

For Recorder and Cello.

Composed in 1988–89.

Dedication: "For H.B. + H.B., with love"

First public performance: July 2, 1997, St. Catherine's Church, Port Erin, Isle of Man, John Turner (Recorder), Jonathan Price (Cello).

Duration: 6 minutes.

Editor's Note: The recorder part has been printed exactly as written by the composer; it has not been transposed, which would be at the octave for alto recorder, or at the 4th for the alto flute. Printing the notation at pitch (in C) follows the composer's intention of leaving it up to the preference of the player at which point to alternate instruments.

PREFACE

On December 15, 1988, Leonard Bernstein went to Key West, Florida, for a winter break. While there, he fulfilled a long-standing promise and wrote these *Variations on an Octatonic Scale* for Helena Burton, daughter of his friend Humphrey Burton. Her instrument was the recorder and Mr. Bernstein decided to leave it up to her which recorder to play; in his manuscript he wrote: "Soprano or alto, or both alternately, as preferred."

By January 9, 1989, when Mr. Bernstein flew to Miami for an overnight stay en route to New York, he made a fair copy of these variations. That day, he attended a rehearsal of Michael Tilson Thomas' orchestra the New World Symphony, at first merely observing this young ensemble, then finally leading it himself (in Rimsky Korsakov's *Scheherazade*). That evening there was a get-together for Mr. Bernstein and the orchestra, and these variations were sight-read by three members of the orchestra (cello and flute, assisted by alto flute).

On finishing these variations (the manuscript fair copy is signed and dated "Key West, Fla. Xmas – New Year, '88–89"), Mr. Bernstein immediately rethought them for a larger ensemble; on the short flight from Key West to Miami he managed to write out a larger variant of Variation IV for clarinet and trombone (assisted by E-flat clarinet and trombones 2 & 3). This expanded set of variations became the second movement, "Mixed Doubles," in his *Concerto for Orchestra* (available on rental from Boosey & Hawkes, and in a Deutsche Grammophon recording: the Israel Philharmonic Orchestra, conducted by Leonard Bernstein; DGG 429 231-2 [CD format]). The grouping of pairs of instruments, as well as the playfulness of the idiosyncratic instrumental writing, recalls the second movement in Bartók's *Concerto for Orchestra*.

The octatonic scale of alternating half-steps and whole steps was one of Mr. Bernstein's favorite modes. This particular eight-tone pattern was used in *Dybbuk*, a large ballet score written by Mr. Bernstein for Jerome Robbins and the New York City Ballet (premiered May 16, 1974; available on rental from Boosey & Hawkes, as ballet or as two orchestra suites). At the bottom of the first page of music in the *Variations*, Mr. Bernstein wrote out this scale, outlining the tritone (tonic-dominant) with brackets.

This may *sound* like conjecture, but is actually the way things often happened in Mr. Bernstein's household. In late December 1988, while waiting for Mr. Bernstein to finish his bath before going out for dinner, I played a few Chopin mazurkas on the piano downstairs – more or less directly under his bathtub. The afternoon of the next day, he showed me the *Thema* and *Variations I & II*, which we then played through together, piano 4-hands. He said he'd been haunted all night by Chopin mazurkas! That influence may not be easily audible in these *Variations,* but it is true that he gathered musical ideas from all sources, and lifted them in his own inspired way into new works (in William Schuman's apt phrase) of "wit, charm, and brilliance."

Charles Harmon

LEONARD BERNSTEIN
VARIATIONS ON AN OCTATONIC SCALE

Recorder and Cello

VARIATIONS ON AN OCTATONIC* SCALE

For H.B. + H.B., with love

Leonard Bernstein (1989)

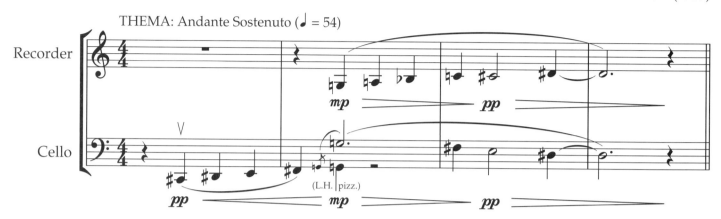

*Scale from *Dybbuk* (1973)

VARIATION I

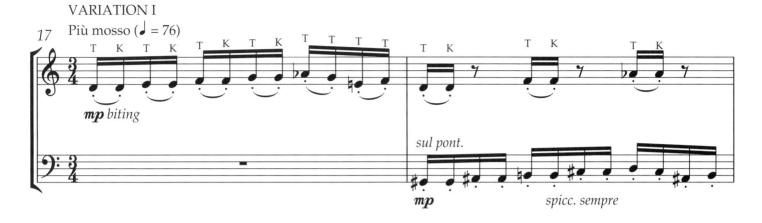

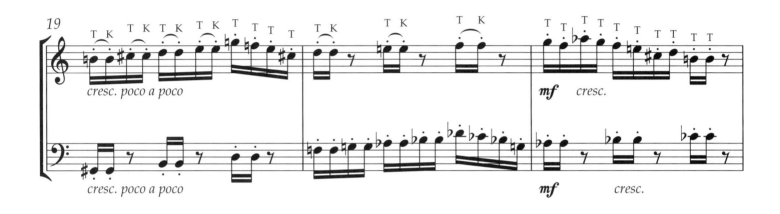

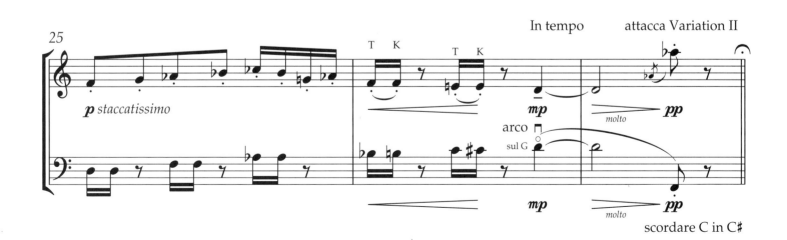

scordare C in C♯

VARIATION II
Più Mosso ma comodo (leisurely Habañera) (♩ = 100, ♩. = 66)

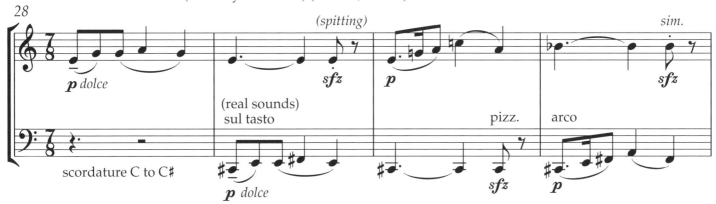

This page is intentionally blank

VARIATION III

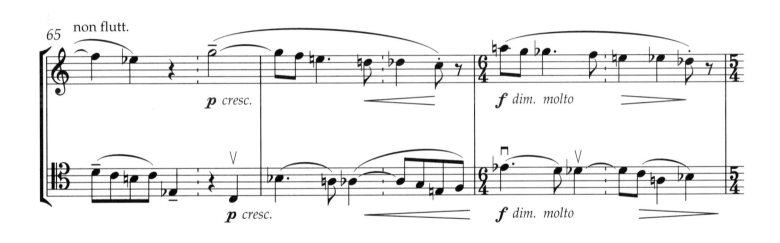

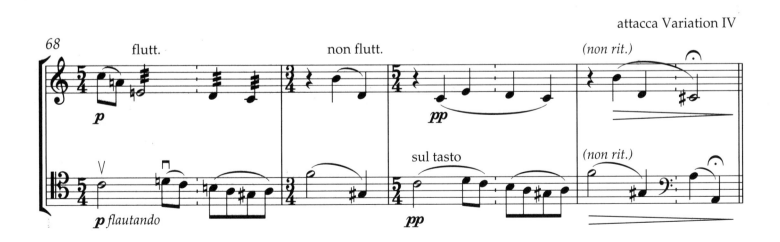

VARIATION IV
Più mosso, quasi allegro (♩ = 132)

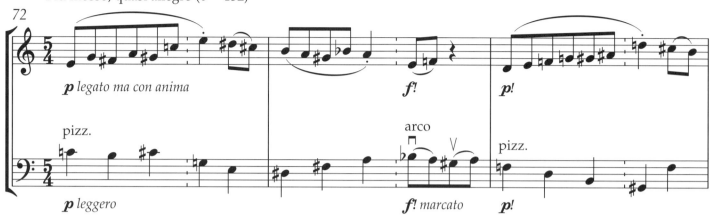

attacca la Coda

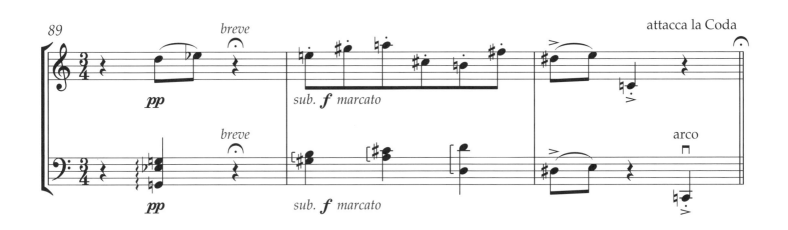

CODA

92 Adagio (♩ = 50-)

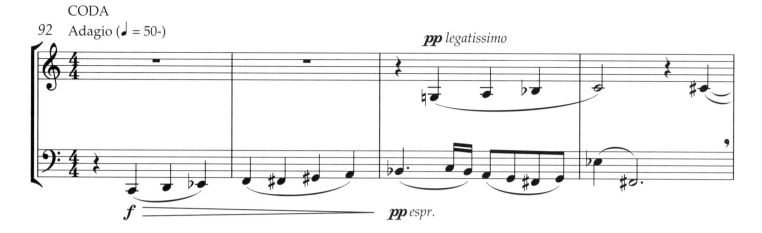

96

99

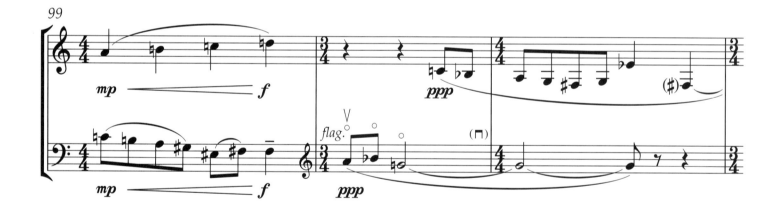

102

* Ossia flageolets

Key West, Fla.
Xmas - New Year, '88-89